A **TRUE** BOOK™

THE EARTH AT RISK

FORESTS IN DANGER

Jasmine Ting

Children's Press®
An imprint of Scholastic Inc.

Content Consultant
Melanie Sturm
Forests and Wildlife Director
Natural Resources Council of Maine

Library of Congress Cataloging-in-Publication Data available
ISBN 978-1-5461-0209-0 (library binding) | ISBN 978-1-5461-0210-6 (paperback) |
ISBN 978-1-5461-0211-3 (ebook)

10 9 8 7 6 5 4 3 2 1   25 26 27 28 29

Printed in China 62
First edition, 2025

Design by Kathleen Petelinsek
Series produced by Spooky Cheetah Press

Front cover: Today, the forest biome is facing several threats, such as deforestation, wildfires, and invasive species, like spotted lanternflies.

Find the Truth!

Everything you are about to read is true *except* for one of the sentences on this page.

Which one is **TRUE**?

T or F   The leaves on all the trees in temperate forests change colors in fall.

T or F   Boreal forests have long winters and short summers.

Find the answers in this book.

What's in This Book?

Most wild Siberian tigers live in the boreal forests of eastern Russia.

Red foxes are found in temperate forests around the world.

The **BIG** Truth

Capturing Carbon

4 Forests Under Threat

The curtain fig tree is found in the rainforests of Australia.

5

INTRODUCTION

A forest is an area with a **large number of trees**. Forests are the **most common** land **biome**—in fact, they cover about **one-third of Earth's surface**. But the world's forests, and all the creatures that live in them, are **under threat** from human activity. Luckily, people are working to save these wild places.

Many plant and animal species in the forest biome are still unknown to science.

The Atlantic Forest is located on the east coast of Brazil in South America. Many of the animals that live there are found nowhere else on Earth.

Forests Around the World

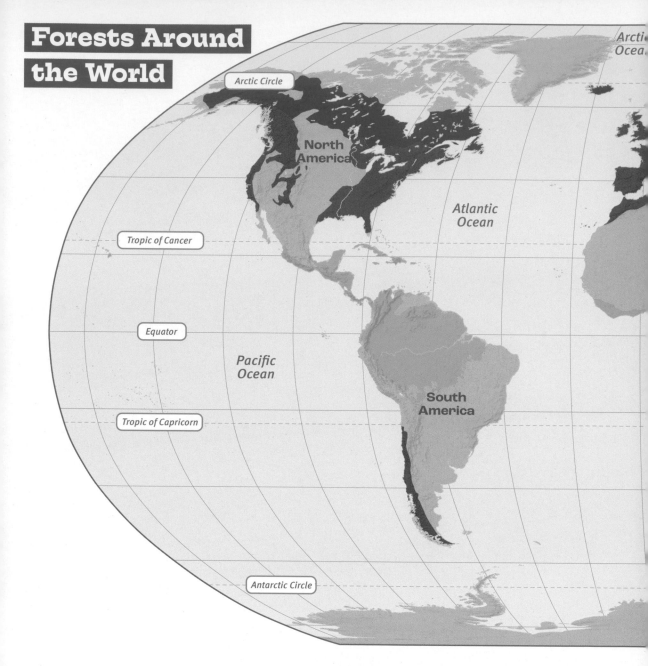

There are three forest **ecosystems**: tropical rainforests, **temperate forests**, and **boreal forests**. Each is found in a different climate. Tropical rainforests are found between the

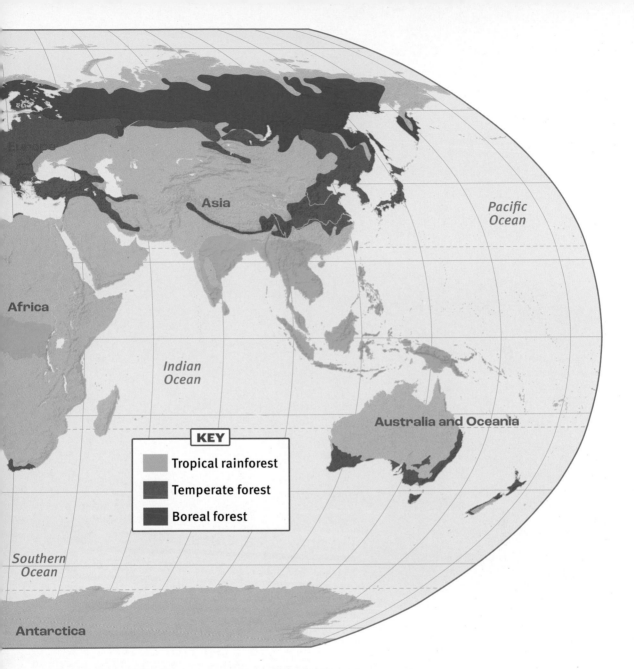

KEY
- Tropical rainforest
- Temperate forest
- Boreal forest

Tropic of Cancer and the Tropic of Capricorn. Temperate forests are found between the tropics and polar regions. Boreal forests exist at higher **latitudes**, just south of the Arctic Circle.

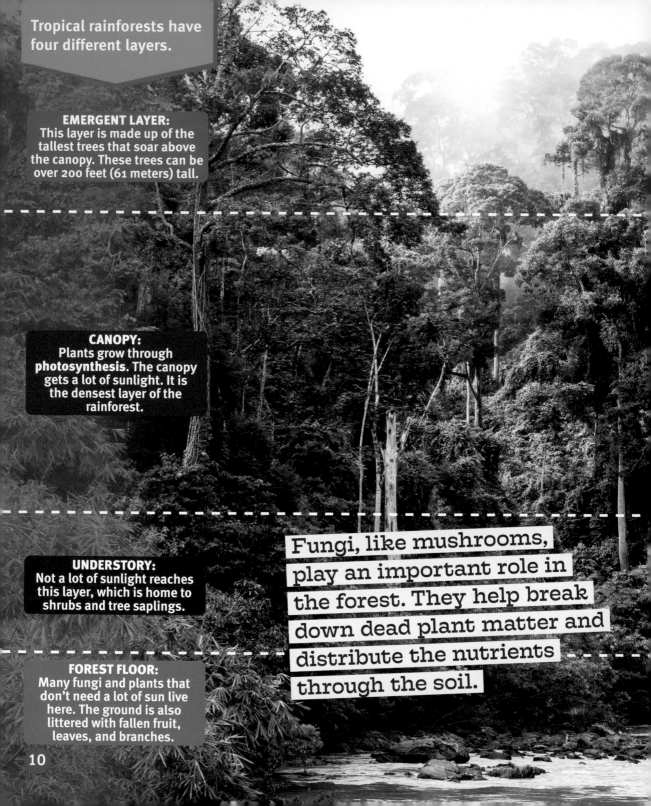

Tropical rainforests have four different layers.

EMERGENT LAYER:
This layer is made up of the tallest trees that soar above the canopy. These trees can be over 200 feet (61 meters) tall.

CANOPY:
Plants grow through **photosynthesis**. The canopy gets a lot of sunlight. It is the densest layer of the rainforest.

UNDERSTORY:
Not a lot of sunlight reaches this layer, which is home to shrubs and tree saplings.

FOREST FLOOR:
Many fungi and plants that don't need a lot of sun live here. The ground is also littered with fallen fruit, leaves, and branches.

Fungi, like mushrooms, play an important role in the forest. They help break down dead plant matter and distribute the nutrients through the soil.

Tropical Rainforests

Tropical rainforests are found in areas with a warm, wet climate. Temperatures stay around 70 degrees to 90° Fahrenheit (21 degrees to 32° Celsius) all year long. This ecosystem experiences two seasons: wet and dry. Each is about six months long. About four times more rain falls during the wet season. Tropical rainforests have some of the highest **biodiversity** of any ecosystem on Earth.

In the Thick of It

Tropical rainforests around the world have their own unique plants. For example, the rainforests of South America are home to tall kapok and Brazil nut trees, as well as the camu camu plant, a shrub with cherry-like fruit that grows in the understory. Fig and beech trees are found in several rainforests, including those in Australia. Bolwarra is a flowering shrub that is found only in Australian rainforests.

kapok tree

Brazil nut tree

fig tree

bolwarra shrub

The canopy is home to epiphytes, such as orchids and bromeliads. Epiphytes are plants that grow on other plants.

The World's Largest Medicine Cabinet

You might be surprised to learn that rainforests are an important source of medicines. In fact, about 25 percent of all modern medicines come from rainforest plants. For example, quinine is a chemical that comes from the bark of cinchona trees. It is used to treat malaria—a deadly disease carried by mosquitoes. Quinine was first discovered by the Quechua People, who live in Peru and Bolivia. A chemical found in the Madagascar periwinkle is used to treat a type of cancer called leukemia.

A man climbs a cinchona tree to harvest bark.

Madagascar periwinkle

South American Animals

South America is home to record-holding rainforest animals. Howler monkeys, which are the loudest monkeys on Earth, live in the canopy. The world's largest spider—the goliath bird-eater tarantula—lives on the forest floor. So does the world's largest rodent—the capybara. River dolphins, caimans, and otters live in or near the Amazon River.

howler monkey

goliath bird-eater tarantula

capybara

river dolphin

About 2.5 million insect species live in the Amazon rainforest in South America.

chimpanzee

bonobo

okapi

crowned eagle

The Congo rainforest is the largest in Africa and the second-largest in the world.

African Animals

Chimpanzees, bonobos, and gorillas all live in the tropical rainforests of Africa. And the Congo rainforest is the only place where okapis are found in the wild. The crowned eagle is one of the top hunters in this ecosystem. Its relatively short wings and long tail help this large bird maneuver through the trees.

Animals of Australia

Many unique animals are found in Australia's rainforests too. The southern cassowary is a large flightless bird. The tree kangaroo has short legs and strong forelimbs that are great for climbing. The sugar glider, a small type of mammal, can soar from tree to tree. This is also where echidnas and platypuses live. They are the only egg-laying mammals on Earth.

tree kangaroo

sugar glider

southern cassowary

echidna

The Daintree rainforest in Australia is the oldest tropical rainforest in the world. Experts say it is about 180 million years old.

two-horned
Sumatran rhino

Malayan
tapir

Sumatran tiger

orangutan

The tropical rainforests on Sumatra are the only place where rhinos, tigers, orangutans, and elephants live together in the wild.

Island Inhabitants

The largest rainforests in Southeast Asia are found on the islands of Borneo and Sumatra. They are home to many animals that are on the brink of extinction. Those include the two-horned Sumatran rhinoceros, the Sumatran tiger, and the Malayan tapir. This is also the only place to find orangutans living in the wild.

spring

The deciduous trees in a temperate forest change with the seasons.

summer

autumn

Trees in a temperate forest have thick bark to protect them from cold winter weather.

18

winter

Temperate Forests

Temperate forests are found in regions that aren't too hot or too cold. This ecosystem experiences all four seasons. And as the weather changes, so do the forest and the creatures that live there. Two types of trees can be found in temperate forests: deciduous and coniferous. The leaves on deciduous trees change color in autumn and start to fall off the tree. Coniferous trees, also called evergreens, stay green year-round.

Falling Leaves

Oak and elm are two examples of deciduous trees. They have thin, wide leaves that are green in summer. In fall, when there is less sunlight and the air is cooler, the leaves change to shades of red, yellow, and orange. They dry up and fall off as the season progresses. In winter, the trees are bare. But the tree isn't dead. New leaves will start to grow in spring.

spring

summer

An oak tree looks different throughout the year.

winter

fall

pine

spruce

fir

A forest of longleaf pines

Conifers have been around for about 300 million years. They were the dominant plant when dinosaurs roamed Earth.

Evergreens

Evergreens, like pine, fir, and spruce trees, are found in temperate forests around the world. They have needle-like leaves. They also have cones. That is why they are called conifers. A forest with mostly evergreens is called a coniferous temperate forest.

Stay or Go?

Animals in a temperate forest **adapt** to the changing seasons. Some, like bears and hedgehogs, eat as much food as they can in spring and summer. Then they **hibernate** in winter. Others, like warblers, swallows, and robins, **migrate** to warmer regions in winter.

black bear

hedgehog

Animals that hibernate can double in size by the end of summer. They will lose up to half of their body weight in winter.

warbler

swallow

fox

rabbit

white-tailed deer

great horned owl

Hidden Creatures

Other creatures in this ecosystem, like deer, foxes, rabbits, and owls, don't hibernate. But they still eat a lot in spring and summer because there will be less food in winter. During cold winter months, the animals become less active to conserve energy. They also grow thicker coats and find hidden shelter to stay warm.

Boreal forests are also known as *taiga*. That means "land of the little sticks" in Russian.

This boreal forest has a mix of evergreens and deciduous trees.

Boreal Forests

Boreal forests grow in high-latitude areas where winter lasts from six to eight months every year. During these snowy months, the temperature ranges from about −65° to −30°F (−54° to −34°C). That is much colder than the temperature in your freezer, which is about 0°F! Summers are short and cool, rarely getting warmer than 77°F (25°C). It may not be surprising, then, to learn that in a boreal forest, a layer of soil below the trees' roots remains frozen year-round. This is known as permafrost. Boreal forests also contain more surface fresh water than any other ecosystem.

Contending with the Cold

Coniferous trees like balsam fir, jackpine, and spruce are well suited to this snowy ecosystem. Because they keep their needles year-round, photosynthesis can occur on any sunny day, even in winter. Deciduous trees include white birch, quaking aspen, and balsam poplar. They grow their leaves in spring and summer. In winter their branches are bare.

balsam fir

jackpine

white birch

quaking aspen

Heavy accumulation of snow can break a tree's branches. That is why narrow trees do well in the taiga—the snow doesn't pile up.

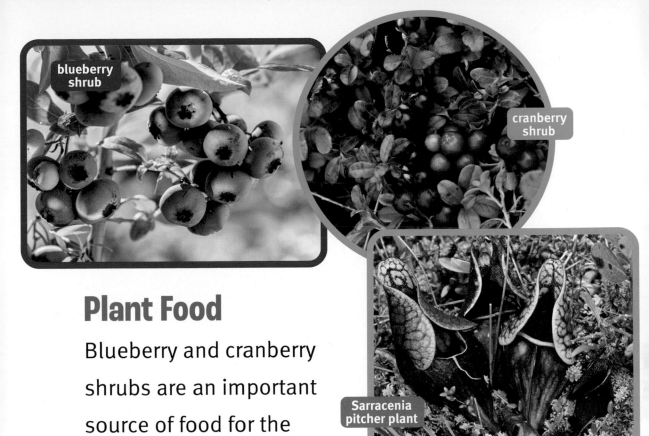

blueberry shrub

cranberry shrub

Sarracenia pitcher plant

Plant Food

Blueberry and cranberry shrubs are an important source of food for the animals in a boreal forest. So are mosses, lichens, and fungi, which don't need a lot of sunlight to survive. The Sarracenia pitcher plant, which can be found in Canada, is an insectivore. Insects fall into liquid in the plant's pitcher and then are digested.

There are 100,000 different types of fungi in the forest biome.

Siberian tiger

moose

gray wolf

snow goose

Creatures of the Cold

The largest cat in the world, the Siberian tiger, can be found in Russia's boreal forests. Other animals are common in this ecosystem around the globe. Those include wolves, moose, and beavers. There are also more than 300 species of birds that rely on these forests for breeding. Species of geese, woodpeckers, and warblers are just some examples.

Life in the Water

Many fish species have adapted to life in the cold waters of the boreal forests. Freshwater fish like pike, trout, and carp may live here year-round. Some fish, like Chinook salmon, are born in small streams in the boreal forest. Then they migrate to the ocean. They return to the forest to reproduce.

pike

trout

salmon

Fish in boreal forests are an important food source for hunters such as bears and bald eagles.

Capturing Carbon

Forests preserve biodiversity. They also provide us with oxygen and other resources, like wood, food, and medicine. Forests are also responsible for most of the carbon sequestration that happens on our planet. That means they are capable of removing carbon from the atmosphere and storing it where it can't easily escape. That helps slow down **climate change**. This is how it happens.

1

Carbon dioxide (CO_2) is released into the atmosphere mainly when we burn fossil fuels like coal and oil to create energy.

2

Trees absorb CO_2 and release oxygen (O_2) into the atmosphere during photosynthesis. During this process, carbon gets stored—or sequestered—in the tree's trunk, branches, leaves, and roots.

O_2

Humans, as well as most living things, need oxygen to live. About 30 percent of the oxygen we breathe comes from trees.

3

CO_2

When a tree or part of a tree dies and falls to the ground, fungi and other organisms break it down. Some of the carbon that was stored in the tree is released into the atmosphere. The rest of the stored carbon gets sequestered in the soil. This sequestration is most effective in boreal forests because the carbon gets locked in permafrost.

C

Around 15 billion trees are chopped down each year around the world.

The trees in this huge section of the Amazon rainforest have been cut down.

Forests Under Threat

Today, forest ecosystems around the world are at risk. Human activities such as deforestation harm forests. Climate change makes wildfires more powerful than ever before. That is why many plants and animals that live in forests are **endangered**. Many forest ecosystems no longer look or function the way they used to, and some have been completely destroyed. People are now taking action to save this crucial biome.

Deforestation

Deforestation is the act of clearing a forest. It is one of the biggest threats to forest health. For thousands of years, humans have cut down trees to clear the land for agriculture. They have also harvested the wood to build homes and furniture, to make paper, and to burn for heat.

This land was cleared for agriculture—to plant crops.

Stewards of the Forest

About 35 percent of the world's remaining intact forests exist on lands inhabited by **Indigenous peoples**. The Yanomami and Kayapo Peoples live in the Amazon rainforest. The Korowai People live in the Papua forests of Indonesia. And there are more than 600 Indigenous communities in Canada's boreal forests. Many of the people who live in these forests play an important role in conserving them. They live in balance with nature, using the resources the forest has to offer respectfully.

Some members of Indigenous communities patrol the forests to keep them safe. This protected forest is in northern Cambodia.

Invasive Species

Invasive species are non-native organisms that compete with native species or even kill them. They are usually introduced by people. The emerald ash borer (EAB) is an insect that is native to Asia. It was accidentally brought to North America in wood that was used to ship products. EABs do not cause a lot of harm to healthy ash trees in Asia. However, they are responsible for killing many trees in North America.

Invasive species can be plants, animals—even germs.

emerald ash borer

EABs feed on the bark and leaves of ash trees.

strawberry guava

Spotted lanternflies are native to parts of Southeast Asia. They were first seen in the United States in 2014 and have caused damage to local plants and trees.

Strawberry guava was first brought to Madagascar from Brazil in 1806. It was planted for food. Strawberry guava harms the rainforest in Madagascar because it grows in dense thickets that push out other vegetation.

Today climate change has created new ways for invasive species to move to different habitats. For example, as a habitat grows warmer, species that couldn't live there before move in.

Uncontrolled Burns

Rising temperatures and droughts are two impacts of climate change. Both dry out the landscape, making it easier for wildfires to catch and spread. Although fire is a natural part of a forest's life cycle, so-called "fire seasons" have become longer and more frequent. And fires have become more intense.

About 70 percent of fire-related tree loss in the past 20 years has happened in boreal forests.

Timeline: Forests Under Pressure

420 MILLION– 360 MILLION YEARS AGO
The very first trees appear on Earth during what scientists call the Devonian period.

10,000 YEARS AGO (8,000 BCE)
Fifty-seven percent of Earth's land is covered by forests.

5,000 YEARS AGO (3,000 BCE)
Civilizations in China, Egypt, Mesopotamia, and the Indus Valley start clearing relatively small portions of land to plant crops. Forest coverage decreases by about 2 percent.

1700
More people begin converting land to farms. By this time, forest coverage has decreased by 5 percent.

Working Together

People are trying to change the future for forests. And they are succeeding. Today, about 21 percent of forests around the globe are protected by laws. In 2021, more than 100 world leaders at the United Nations 26th Climate Change Conference promised to end and reverse deforestation by 2030. Together, we can all work toward a brighter future for our forests—and for us!

1800
Advances in technology make it easier to convert forested land to agriculture. Forest coverage decreases by an additional 2 percent from the 1700s.

1900
Forest coverage decreases by an additional 2 percent since the 1800s.

2010
In the previous 30 years, 420 million hectares of forest were lost. That's an area larger than India.

TODAY
The planet has lost almost half of its forests. Coverage has decreased from 57 percent to about 30 percent.

Amazing Comeback

From the 1970s to the 1990s, thousands of trees in Kenya, a country in Africa, were cut down to make room for farms and to harvest timber among other things. This affected the livelihood of many women in the country who depended on the forests as a source of firewood for cooking and logs to make fences. It was also where they gathered plants and caught animals to eat.

In 1977, Professor Wangari Maathai began an organization called the Green Belt Movement (GBM) to help Kenyan women and restore forests in the country. Professor Maathai gave the women seedlings and tree saplings to plant,

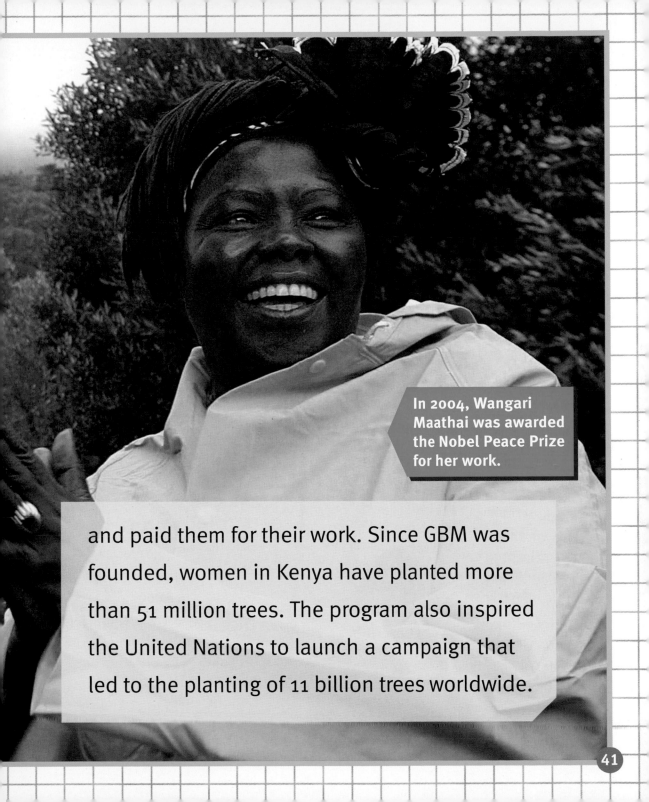

In 2004, Wangari Maathai was awarded the Nobel Peace Prize for her work.

and paid them for their work. Since GBM was founded, women in Kenya have planted more than 51 million trees. The program also inspired the United Nations to launch a campaign that led to the planting of 11 billion trees worldwide.

Kid Heroes

Jack Dalton is known as "The Kid Conservationist." That means he's helping to protect animals, plants, and the planet. When Jack was eight years old, he learned about deforestation and how it was destroying the home of his favorite animal, the orangutan. So in 2019, he started making YouTube videos and spreading awareness about the dangers our environment is facing.

1

Q: What do you do as "the Kid Conservationist"?

A: A big part of my conservation work is education. I do presentations to kids of all ages—about orangutans, the rainforest, and a lot of different things. Education is the first step. If we don't know about an issue, how can we help it? And once we educate people, that's how they can take action toward becoming conservationists themselves.

2

Q: What is your favorite project that you've worked on?

A: I have a children's book, and I've sold nearly 3,000 copies. For every book sold, a tree is planted in the Indonesian rainforest. The book is about baby orangutans, the special relationship they have with their mothers, and how important they are to the rest of the rainforest ecosystem.

3

Q: What message do you have for kids who want to help save forests?

A: There are a lot of changes we can make to our everyday lives—including something as simple as using less paper. Learning more about forests and how to save them is important. So is sharing that information with others. I want kids to remember that they can have a big impact on the planet. It's important that they help protect our rainforests—and our world—for future generations.

True Statistics*

Number of tree species found in the world's forests: More than 70,000

Percentage of land animals and plants that are found in forests: More than 80%

Height of the world's tallest living tree: 380.3 feet (115.9 m)—Hyperion, a redwood, found in California, U.S.A.

Area of the world's largest forest: Around 2.7 million square miles (6.9 million sq. km)—the Amazon rainforest in South America

Size of forest areas lost each year: About 10 million hectares, which is roughly the size of South Korea

Number of people that depend on forests for their living: More than 1.6 billion

As of 2024

Did you find the truth?

F The leaves on all the trees in temperate forests change colors in fall.

T Boreal forests have long winters and short summers.

Resources

Other books in this series:

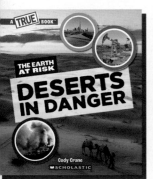 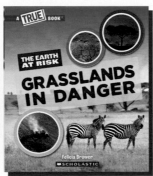  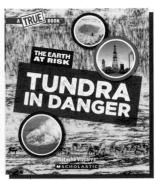

You can also look at:

Eboch, Christine Elizabeth. *Forest Biomes Around the World*. New York: Capstone, 2019.

McDaniel, Melissa. *Understanding Climate Change: Facing a Warming World*. New York: Scholastic, 2020.

Nargi, Lela. *Forest Biomes*. Minneapolis, MN: Jump!, 2022.

Vonder Brink, Tracy. *Protecting the Amazon Rainforest*. Mendota Heights, MN: Focus Readers, 2020.

Glossary

adapt (uh-DAPT) to change to suit a different situation

biodiversity (bye-oh-duh-VUR-si-tee) the condition of nature in which a wide variety of species live in a single area

biome (BYE-ohm) a region of the world with similar animals and plants

climate change (KLYE-mit CHAYNJ) global warming and other changes in the weather and weather patterns that are happening because of human activity

ecosystems (EE-koh-sis-tuhmz) all the living things in a place and their relation to the environment

endangered (en-DAYN-jurd) in danger of becoming extinct, usually because of human activity

hibernate (HYE-bur-nate) to spend the winter in a sleeping or resting state

Indigenous peoples (in-DI-juh-nuhs PEE-puhlz) the first known inhabitants of a place

latitudes (LAT-i-toodz) regions marked by their latitude, which is the distance north or south of the equator, measured in degrees

migrate (MYE-grate) to move to another area or climate at a particular time of year

photosynthesis (foh-toh-SIN-thi-sis) a chemical process by which plants and some other organisms make their food

Index

Page numbers in **bold** indicate illustrations.

About the Author

Jasmine Ting is a Filipino journalist based in New York City. Her work has been published in magazines, including *Scholastic News*. She enjoys telling stories about important events, recent trends, and people doing amazing things around the globe. She hopes her writing inspires young readers to learn more about the world around them. *Forests in Danger* is Jasmine's second book. Her first book was a True Book entitled *Green Energy*.